11/11

P9-AQG-207

Allen County Public Library

REMARKABLE
PEOPLE

Aung San
Suu Kyi

by Simon Rose

www.av2books.com

Go to **www.av2books.com,** and enter this book's unique code.

BOOK CODE

L913622

AV² by Weigl brings you media enhanced books that support active learning.

AV² provides enriched content that supplements and complements this book. Weigl's AV² books strive to create inspired learning and engage young minds in a total learning experience.

Your AV² Media Enhanced books come alive with...

Audio
Listen to sections of the book read aloud.

Video
Watch informative video clips.

Embedded Weblinks
Gain additional information for research.

Try This!
Complete activities and hands-on experiments.

Key Words
Study vocabulary, and complete a matching word activity.

Quizzes
Test your knowledge.

Slide Show
View images and captions, and prepare a presentation.

... and much, much more!

Published by AV² by Weigl
350 5th Avenue, 59th Floor
New York, NY 10118

www.av2books.com   www.weigl.com

Copyright ©2012 AV² by Weigl

All rights reserved. No part of this publication may be reproduced, stored in a retrieval system, or transmitted in any form or by any means, electronic, mechanical, photocopying, recording, or otherwise, without the prior written permission of the publisher.

Library of Congress Cataloging-in-Publication Data

Rose, Simon, 1961-
  Aung San Suu Kyi / Simon Rose.
    p. cm. -- (Remarkable people)
  Includes index.
  ISBN 978-1-61690-833-1 (hardcover : alk. paper) -- ISBN 978-1-61690-834-8 (softcover : alk. paper)
  1. Aung San Suu Kyi--Juvenile literature. 2. Women political activists--Burma--Biography--Juvenile literature. 3. Political activists--Burma--Biography--Juvenile literature. 4. Women political prisoners--Burma--Biography--Juvenile literature. 5. Burma--Politics and government--1948---Juvenile literature. 6. Democracy--Burma--Juvenile literature. I. Title.
  DS530.53.A85R67 2012
  959.105092--dc22
  [B]
                            2011011584

Printed in the United States of America in North Mankato, Minnesota
1 2 3 4 5 6 7 8 9 0 15 14 13 12 11

WEP37500
052011

Editor: Heather Kissock
Design: Terry Paulhus

Photograph Credits
Weigl acknowledges Getty Images as the primary image supplier for this title.

Every reasonable effort has been made to trace ownership and to obtain permission to reprint copyright material. The publishers would be pleased to have any errors or omissions brought to their attention so that they may be corrected in subsequent printings.

Contents

Who Is Aung San Suu Kyi?

Aung San Suu Kyi is an **activist** in Myanmar, the Southeast Asian country formerly known as Burma. Myanmar is governed by the country's military, who enforce strict rules on its citizens. People have few rights in Myanmar. Those who disagree with the government are often arrested and put in prison.

Suu Kyi has fought to make her country a **democracy**. She wants her people to have more rights and more choice in how the country is run. She helped found the National League for Democracy. This group has worked toward making Myanmar a democratic country.

The military government has not supported Suu Kyi's fight for democracy. She has been placed under **house arrest** several times for speaking out against the government. Despite her imprisonment, she has always kept working toward democracy, freedom, and **human rights** in her country. As a result of this work, she was awarded the **Nobel Peace Prize** in 1991.

"Tyranny does not crumble by itself. Freedom must be demanded and defended, by those who have been denied it and those who are already free."

Growing Up

Aung San Suu Kyi was born in Rangoon, Burma, on June 19, 1945. She was the youngest of three children and the only daughter of Aung San and Daw Khin Kyi. When Suu Kyi was born, Burma was part of the **British Empire**. Many Burmese people, including Aung San, did not like being under British rule. Like his daughter, Aung San became an activist. He fought for Burma's independence from Great Britain. In July 1947, however, Aung San was **assassinated**. He never saw his country gain its independence from the British Empire on January 4, 1948.

Daw Khin Kyi worked with her husband in the fight for independence. The couple often hosted political meetings at their home. Daw Khin Kyi continued to host similar meetings after her husband died. As a result, while growing up, Suu Kyi met and talked with people of many different political beliefs, backgrounds, and religions.

■ Aung San is considered a national hero for his efforts to make Burma an independent country.

Get to Know MYANMAR

COAT OF ARMS

NATIONAL FLAG

NATIONAL BIRD
Burmese Pheasant

0   500 Miles

0   500 Kilometers

Burma was the name of the country until 1989. Then, it officially became known as Myanmar.

Myanmar has an area of 261,391 square miles (677,000 square kilometers).

The official language of Myanmar is Burmese.

The population of Myanmar is about 50 million. The city of Yangon, formerly known as Rangoon, is the largest city. It has a population of about five million.

Myanmar has a long and varied history. It has been ruled by another country and has been governed by its own military. How do you think being born in Myanmar affected Aung San Suu Kyi's personal and political beliefs? How would your life be different if you lived there?

Practice Makes Perfect

After her father's death, Aung San Suu Kyi continued to live in Burma with her mother. However, in 1960, her mother was named Burma's **ambassador** to India and Nepal. The family moved to India, where Suu Kyi continued her high school education. Following graduation, she was accepted into Delhi University. She studied politics there until 1964. She then moved to Great Britain to continue her studies. In 1967, Suu Kyi received a degree in philosophy, politics, and economics from St. Hugh's College at Oxford University.

■ Oxford University is the oldest university in the English-speaking world. It was founded more than 900 years ago.

Two years later, Suu Kyi moved to New York to study for an advanced degree. While there, she stayed with a family friend who worked at the United Nations. Soon, Suu Kyi was offered a position at the United Nations as well. She put her studies on hold to take the job. Suu Kyi left the United Nations in 1972, when she married Michael Aris. The two had met while attending university in Great Britain.

QUICK FACTS

- Suu Kyi is pronounced *Soo Chee*. Her name means "a bright collection of strange victories."

- Like most Burmese, Suu Kyi practices the Buddhist religion.

- Suu Kyi's speeches, writings, and interviews have been published in several books.

Michael was an author and scholar. He was in great demand as a teacher. In the years following their marriage, the couple spent time living and working in Bhutan, Great Britain, and India.

■ Michael Aris died in 1999. Suu Kyi did not attend his funeral. She was afraid that, if she left Burma, she would not be allowed to return.

Key Events

In 1988, Suu Kyi received news that her mother was ill. Suu Kyi returned to Burma to take care of her. At that time, Ne Win, the head of the military, stepped down from his position as ruler of the country. It was a time of change for Burma. People began to protest against military rule. Mass **demonstrations** were held across the country.

Although she had returned to Burma to be with her family, Suu Kyi joined the pro-democracy movement, which was calling for political change in Burma. In September 1988, she helped found a new political party called the National League for Democracy. As one of its leaders, she began **campaigning** for democratic government in Burma. On August 26, 1988, a crowd of about 500,000 gathered in Rangoon to hear her speak.

■ Ne Win was Burma's leader from 1962 to 1988.

Thoughts from Aung San Suu Kyi

Aung San Suu Kyi is passionate about achieving democracy for Myanmar. Here are some of the comments she has made about the struggle to achieve democracy for her country.

Suu Kyi explains why democracy is important to her country.
"The people of Burma are like prisoners in their own country, deprived of all freedom under military rule."

Suu Kyi discusses truth and human understanding.
"Concepts such as truth, justice, and compassion cannot be dismissed as trite when these are often the only bulwarks which stand against ruthless power."

Suu Kyi knows that achieving democracy in Myanmar will take time.
"We have faith in the power to change what needs to be changed but we are under no illusion that the transition from **dictatorship** to liberal democracy will be easy, or that democratic government will mean the end of all our problems."

Suu Kyi comments on corruption in government.
"It is not power that corrupts but fear. Fear of losing power corrupts those who wield it and fear of the scourge of power corrupts those who are subject to it."

Suu Kyi believes in fighting for her beliefs.
"Those of us who decided to work for democracy in Burma made our choice in the conviction that the danger of standing up for basic human rights in a repressive society was preferable to the safety of a quiescent life in servitude."

Suu Kyi relates to her father's earlier fight for independence.
"I could not, as my father's daughter, remain indifferent to what was going on."

What Is an Activist?

An activist works for a cause. The cause may be to solve a problem or to make the world a better place. Political activists, such as Aung San Suu Kyi, seek to bring change to the way people are governed. Other activists may work to protect the environment or help animals. Some activists volunteer for a cause they care about. Others make it a career.

Activists often plan campaigns to draw attention to their cause. Sometimes, campaigns are aimed at improving people's knowledge of an issue. These are called public awareness campaigns. Other campaigns might urge people to take specific actions. Suu Kyi held peaceful demonstrations in public areas to get her party's message to the public. At these demonstrations, she spoke to people about the need for democracy in her country and how it would benefit their lives.

■ Activists, such as Suu Kyi, often speak to the media to promote their cause and get their message to a wider audience.

Activists 101

Nelson Mandela (1918–)

In the 1960s, Nelson Mandela was a leading member of the African National Congress (ANC). This group fought against **apartheid** in South Africa. Mandela's fight for black freedom led to his imprisonment in 1962. After his release from prison in 1990, Mandela worked with South Africa's president to end apartheid peacefully. For their efforts, the men were awarded the Nobel Peace Prize in 1993. Shortly after winning this award, Mandela was elected president of South Africa. He stayed in this position until his retirement in 1999.

Stephen Biko (1946–1977)

Stephen Biko was a South African anti-apartheid activist in the 1960s and 1970s. He first became involved in politics as a student leader. Biko was the Founder of the Black Consciousness Movement. This was a political movement that took place in the mid-1960s. Biko died in police custody due to mistreatment.

Martin Luther King Jr. (1929–1968)

At the age of 28, Martin Luther King, Jr. helped form the Southern Christian Leadership Conference (SCLC) to fight for the **civil rights** of African Americans. He led demonstrations and marches throughout the United States to bring his cause to the public. King's most famous speech, "I Have a Dream," took place during the 1963 March on Washington. During the march, 250,000 people marched to Washington, D.C. to mark the 100th anniversary of the ending of slavery in the United States. On April 4, 1968, following a speech in Memphis, Tennessee, King was assassinated.

Ch'iu Chin (1879–1907)

Ch'iu Chin was a Chinese **revolutionary**. She dared to speak out against the powerful emperors who ruled China. She even formed secret societies to try to overthrow them. Ch'iu was captured and tortured, but she refused to confess to any crimes. She was then beheaded. The Chinese honor her as one of their great heroes.

Burma (Myanmar)

Almost 1,000 years ago, Burma was an independent kingdom. Later, it was conquered by other nations. In the 19th century, it became part of the British Empire. During World War II, Japan gained control of Burma. After Japan's defeat in the war, the British again ruled Burma. In 1948, however, Burma became an independent country. It was run as a democracy until 1962 when a group of army officers seized power. Since then, Burma has been ruled by a military council that allows no opposition. The country's name was changed to Myanmar in 1989.

Influences

Aung San Suu Kyi has been greatly influenced by Mohandas Gandhi. Gandhi is most famous as the non-violent leader of India's fight for independence, leading protests and demonstrations against British rule from the 1920s until 1948. However, Gandhi's work actually began in South Africa in the earlier part of the 20th century when he protested against the **racial discrimination** suffered by Indians living there. On his return to India, Gandhi gradually developed his methods of non-violent protest known as *satyagraha*. This word means "insistence on truth."

■ Gandhi's methods of non-violent protest have inspired many civil rights activists throughout the world.

As a Buddhist, Suu Kyi draws inspiration from her religious beliefs and also from the Dalai Lama. He is the Buddhist spiritual leader of the people of Tibet. The people of Tibet have struggled to win their independence from Chinese rule for half a century. The Dalai Lama has quietly supported this struggle. As a result, he was forced to leave Tibet and has lived in **exile** in India for more than 50 years. In 1989, he was awarded the Nobel Peace Prize for his work in attempting to bring freedom to his people.

Aung San Suu Kyi's Family

Aung San Suu Kyi has drawn much support from her family. This includes her husband and two sons. Michael Aris traveled worldwide accepting awards for his wife and **lobbying** for her cause. When he died in 1999, their sons Alexander and Kim continued working internationally on their mother's behalf.

■ In November 2010, Kim Aris arrived in Myanmar to visit his mother. It was the first time in 10 years that he had seen her. He had been denied entry into the country on previous attempts.

Overcoming Obstacles

Shortly before Aung San Suu Kyi helped create the National League for Democracy in 1988, the State Law and Order Restoration Council seized control of the country. Political gatherings were banned. Suu Kyi defied the ban and toured the country making pro-democracy speeches. On July 20, 1989, Suu Kyi was placed under house arrest for the first time. She was offered her freedom if she agreed to leave the country, but she refused. She suspected that she would never be allowed to return.

When she was released in 1995, the government still kept her under close control. She was not allowed to travel outside the city of Yangon. Despite these restrictions, she continued her work to try to bring freedom and democracy to her country.

■ While under house arrest, Suu Kyi was limited to her house and gardens. She spent much of her time reading and listening to news on the radio.

In September 2000, Suu Kyi was again placed under house arrest for trying to travel to another city without permission. She was released in May 2002. As she had done before, Suu Kyi resumed her campaigning for the people of Myanmar. This time, she was allowed to travel outside Yangon. She spoke to large crowds wherever she went. Following more unrest in the country, she was returned to house arrest in May 2003.

Suu Kyi's long years of house arrest and her isolation from her family and the outside world have been difficult. Yet, to the long-suffering people of Myanmar, she has remained a symbol of resistance to the military **regime**. Suu Kyi was most recently released from house arrest in November 2010.

■ A crowd of thousands gathered to see Suu Kyi after her release from house arrest in November 2010.

Achievements and Successes

Aung San Suu Kyi was awarded the Nobel Peace Prize in 1991 for her work in trying to bring democracy to Myanmar. Unable to accept the award herself due to her continuing house arrest, her sons accepted the award on her behalf. Suu Kyi used the $1.3 million prize money to set up a health and education trust for the people of Myanmar. Many countries have called for her release over the years and continue to support Suu Kyi in her struggle for democracy.

■ The Nobel Peace Prize is one of five Nobel Prizes. The awards are named after Swedish inventor Alfred Nobel. The first peace prize was awarded in 1901.

Suu Kyi has received a number of other awards. These include the Congressional Gold Medal and the Presidential Medal of Freedom from the United States and the International Simon Bolivar Prize from the United Nations and Venezuela. These awards were given to her for her efforts toward establishing democracy in her country. Suu Kyi was also granted honorary Canadian citizenship in 2007. Only five people have ever been given this honor.

HELPING OTHERS

Suu Kyi has worked hard to help the people of Myanmar in their struggle for democracy, but she has provided for them in other ways as well. The health and education trust she set up with her Nobel Peace Prize money ensures that money is available for health care and schooling. The trust acts as a charity, giving money to those who need it most.

Write a Biography

A person's life story can be the subject of a book. This kind of book is called a biography. Biographies describe the lives of remarkable people, such as those who have achieved great success or have done important things to help others. These people may be alive today, or they may have lived many years ago. Reading a biography can help you learn more about a remarkable person.

At school, you might be asked to write a biography. First, decide who you want to write about. You can choose an activist, such as Aung San Suu Kyi, or any other person. Then, find out if your library has any books about this person. Learn as much as you can about him or her. Write down the key events in this person's life. What was this person's childhood like? What has he or she accomplished? What are his or her goals? What makes this person special or unusual?

A concept web is a useful research tool. Read the questions in the following concept web. Answer the questions in your notebook. Your answers will help you write a biography.

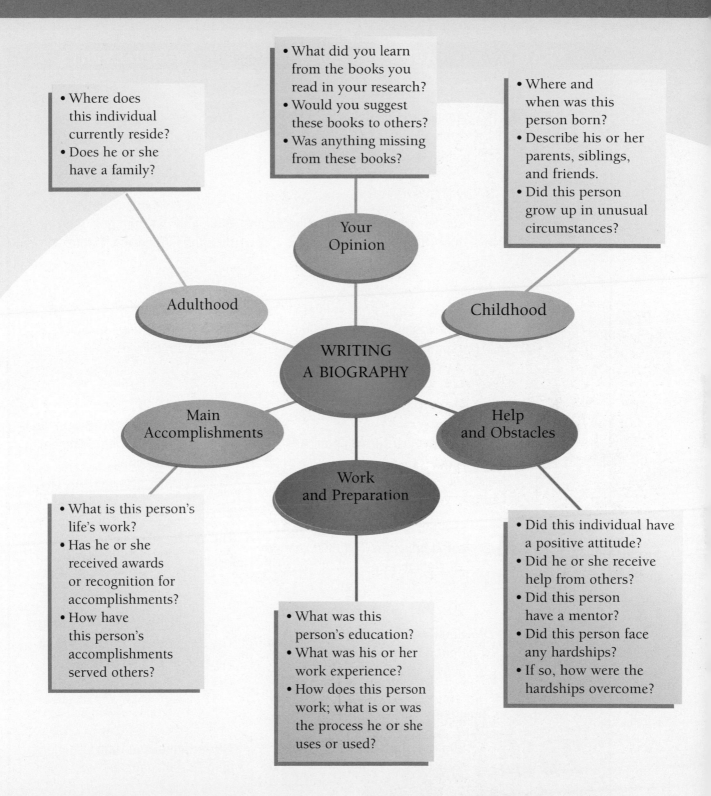

- Where does this individual currently reside?
- Does he or she have a family?

- What did you learn from the books you read in your research?
- Would you suggest these books to others?
- Was anything missing from these books?

- Where and when was this person born?
- Describe his or her parents, siblings, and friends.
- Did this person grow up in unusual circumstances?

Your Opinion

Adulthood

Childhood

WRITING A BIOGRAPHY

Main Accomplishments

Help and Obstacles

Work and Preparation

- What is this person's life's work?
- Has he or she received awards or recognition for accomplishments?
- How have this person's accomplishments served others?

- What was this person's education?
- What was his or her work experience?
- How does this person work; what is or was the process he or she uses or used?

- Did this individual have a positive attitude?
- Did he or she receive help from others?
- Did this person have a mentor?
- Did this person face any hardships?
- If so, how were the hardships overcome?

Timeline

YEAR	AUNG SAN SUU KYI	WORLD EVENTS
1945	Aung San Suu Kyi is born on June 19.	The Second World War comes to an end.
1947	Suu Kyi's father is assassinated on July 19.	India and Pakistan gain their independence from Britain.
1964	Suu Kyi begins her studies in philosophy, politics, and economics at Oxford University in Great Britain.	Martin Luther King, Jr. wins the Nobel Peace Prize.
1972	Suu Kyi marries Michael Aris.	U.S. President Richard Nixon visits China and meets with Communist leader Mao Zedong.
1988	Suu Kyi returns to Burma and helps found the National League for Democracy.	The Winter Olympics take place in Calgary, Alberta, Canada.
1991	Suu Kyi is awarded the Nobel Peace Prize while under house arrest.	The Soviet Union breaks up into a number of independent states.
2010	Suu Kyi is released from house arrest in November.	An earthquake in Haiti kills more than 230,000 people.

Words to Know

activist: a person who takes action to achieve political goals

ambassador: someone who represents his or her country in another country

apartheid: a system of racial segregation imposed by the South African government until 1994

assassinated: murdered a prominent person

British Empire: a grouping of people and land ruled by Great Britain

campaigning: engaging in a series of activities that work toward a goal

civil rights: the basic rights guaranteed to the citizens of a country

democracy: a form of government in which power comes from the people

demonstrations: public displays of group opinions

dictatorship: absolute, overbearing control

exile: forced to live in another country

house arrest: kept under guard in their own home and not allowed to communicate with the outside world

human rights: the basic freedoms to which all people are entitled

lobbying: trying to influence the thinking of public officials

Nobel Peace Prize: awarded every year since 1901 to a person who has worked to promote peace

racial discrimination: the act of treating someone unfairly because of his or her race

regime: a form of government

revolutionary: a person who fights for change

Index

Log on to www.av2books.com

AV² by Weigl brings you media enhanced books that support active learning. Go to www.av2books.com, and enter the special code found on page 2 of this book. You will gain access to enriched and enhanced content that supplements and complements this book. Content includes video, audio, web links, quizzes, a slide show, and activities.

Audio
Listen to sections of the book read aloud.

Video
Watch informative video clips.

Embedded Weblinks
Gain additional information for research.

Try This!
Complete activities and hands-on experiments.

WHAT'S ONLINE?

Try This!	Embedded Weblinks	Video	EXTRA FEATURES
Complete an activity about your childhood.	Learn more about Suu Kyi's life.	Watch a video about Suu Kyi.	
Try this activity about key events.	More information on Suu Kyi's achievments and awards.	Check out another video about Suu Kyi.	
Complete an activity about overcoming obstacles.	Check out a site about Suu Kyi.		
Write a biography.			
Try this timeline activity.			

 Audio
Listen to sections of the book read aloud.

 Key Words
Study vocabulary, and complete a matching word activity.

 Slide Show
View images and captions, and prepare a presentation.

 Quizzes
Test your knowledge.

AV² was built to bridge the gap between print and digital. We encourage you to tell us what you like and what you want to see in the future.

Sign up to be an AV² Ambassador at www.av2books.com/ambassador.

Due to the dynamic nature of the Internet, some of the URLs and activities provided as part of AV² by Weigl may have changed or ceased to exist. AV² by Weigl accepts no responsibility for any such changes. All media enhanced books are regularly monitored to update addresses and sites in a timely manner. Contact AV² by Weigl at 1-866-649-3445 or av2books@weigl.com with any questions, comments, or feedback.